GENGIS AMONGST
THE PYGMIES

Gregory Motton

GENGIS AMONGST THE PYGMIES

OBERON BOOKS

LONDON

First published in 2003 by Oberon Books Ltd.
(incorporating Absolute Classics)
521 Caledonian Road, London N7 9RH
Tel: 020 7607 3637 / Fax: 020 7607 3629
e-mail: oberon.books@btinternet.com
www.oberonbooks.com

A catalogue record for this book is available from the British
Library.

ISBN: 9781840023466

Cover design: Andrzej Klimowski

Characters

GENGIS

AUNTY

UNCLE

ANNIE

MAURICE PORKER

MR WHEREYABINHIDIN'

THUMBELINA

SOUL PRESTIGE

VICKY SLIMMING

PART ONE

I

GENGIS is standing on a chair with a rope around his neck.

AUNTY: Do you want the good news or the bad news first?

GENGIS: The good news.

AUNTY: Capital punishment has just been abolished.

GENGIS: And the bad news?

AUNTY: Capital-ism has just been extended…indefinitely. You may have to stay there forever. But we can change the chair every few minutes to a more modern design that expresses your personality better.

GENGIS: Well I'm delighted. Can I make a speech?

AUNTY: Of course. Freedom of speech is not just a necessity, it's a must-have.

GENGIS: Can I say anything I like?

AUNTY: Why surely. As Henry Ford once said, you can have any opinion you like as long as it's one we already have in stock.

GENGIS: Right.

AUNTY: The other good news is you've just won the competition to be leader of this once great nation of ours.

GENGIS: Aha!

AUNTY: Yes, you'll be in charge of stocking the shelves, and marketing outreach policy mission statement. We expect great things of you.

GENGIS: I can see that. The world is an oyster! Yippee! Can I start now?

AUNTY: Start whenever you like – it won't make a blind bit of difference.

GENGIS: (*Gets down.*) Right then you bastards. So. Let's see if we can get any sense out of you this time around.

AUNTY: Yes Gengis.

GENGIS: First of all – where's Uncle?

AUNTY: He's outside gathering a new mandate from the people, on your behalf.

GENGIS: Before he comes, Aunty, I want to make a confession.

AUNTY: Of course dear.

GENGIS: I now realise that I got it completely wrong last time.

AUNTY: Oh no…

GENGIS: Oh yes! I was too hard…

AUNTY: Yes. Perhaps…

GENGIS: …and yet too soft at the same time.

AUNTY: What will you do this time?

GENGIS: The opposite.

AUNTY: Oh.

GENGIS: Yes, you see, I don't think I really got the idea across properly.

AUNTY: Oh no!

GENGIS: Oh yes! I failed to make the point…clearly enough. This time, I shall bludgeon them with subtlety until they are screaming out for clarity, and I shall tantalise them with clarity until they are demanding subtlety. I shall agree with everyone, and they shall agree with me. I shall be rich, and you, Aunty, shall be my spokesperson. Promotion for everyone. Hurrah!

AUNTY: Hurrah! A big promotion!

GENGIS: (*He spies UNCLE loitering in the doorway.*) Uncle, what are you doing loitering at my entrance? Come in at once! This is no time for being withdrawn. We are open to all. It's a new beginning.

UNCLE: That is music to my deafened ears, a sight for sore eyes, a cloud lifting from my eclipse, a nettle removed from my flip-flop, oil released from my swollen tanker, All hail Lady Jesus!

GENGIS: Uncle, you're drunk.

UNCLE: I've been celebrating your return to power. Such emotion. My God how the people have warmed to your warm smile of warmth; behold he is a man of contrasts; he is warm one minute, wet the next...

GENGIS: I have an announcement to make; you know how Napoleon said the British were a nation of shoplifters [*sic.*] –

AUNTY: Did he? The cheek!

GENGIS: Well, I'm going to rid us of the stigma once and for all; instead we shall become a nation of shopfitters.

AUNTY: You mean –

GENGIS: Yes, we're going to modernise the shop.

AUNTY/UNCLE: (*Together.*) Modernise the shop??

GENGIS: Yes, rip out the counter.

AUNTY: But we ripped the counter out already.

GENGIS: Then rip it out again! Tear out the antique windows!

UNCLE: It's been done. Years ago.

GENGIS: Then do it again. Flatten it! Tear down the walls. I'm going open-plan. I want preservation. Modernise or die!

UNCLE: But Gengis, there's nothing left after last time. It's all long gone.

AUNTY: Yes, what do you mean by modernise?

UNCLE: Built for speed, is that what you mean?

GENGIS: Well, yes, speed or, or, or ppppppppppppprofit.

UNCLE: Ah, now I understand.

GENGIS: But I was wondering... Won't anybody mind?

UNCLE: These days there just isn't anyone who minds. There's nothing to fear anymore Gengis.

AUNTY: Rejoice!

GENGIS: But someone might be in a distant corner of the world cooking up resentment.

UNCLE: No, impossible. You see, from the Taipans of Thailand, from Dagenham to Dagestan, we're all joining hands around a great big bonfire and warming ourselves in the November glow, a twilight roasted milkshake sausage, from prime chicken fat. Whoever doesn't join in is just a Pygmy.

GENGIS: Yes, now what *about* the Pygmies?

UNCLE: Oh, they're very far away, and so small as to be invisible, planted in sweet little rows in their reservations; men of yesterday.

GENGIS: The world is as One.

UNCLE: Yes.

GENGIS: It seems we have friends everywhere. My whole body is experiencing opportunities for growth. I can feel my arse expanding where I sit.

AUNTY: Exciting new vistas are opening up.

GENGIS: It's no good, I can't contain myself anymore. I must away, beyond Dover, beyond Schengen, out to the brown world to share my good fortune. I shall build a monument to providence in the form of a great tower.

UNCLE: And what shall this tower be called O great Khan?

GENGIS: Called? A fucking great big office block is what it shall be called. And I'm going to build one right in the middle of a paddy field.

UNCLE: There's no need to travel, you see, this came in.

GENGIS: What is it?

UNCLE: What is it? It's a computer.

GENGIS: Oh, what does it do?

UNCLE: Everything. It's a school, a library, and a brothel all in one. It'll even suck your cock for you if you want.

GENGIS: Have we really come that far? Where are all the people?

UNCLE: The children, for example, are all inside doing their homework.

GENGIS: They must be very tiny!

UNCLE: They are. Minute! That's what they mean by reducing class sizes. The children are so fucking tiny you can hardly see them anymore. It's marvellous. A whole life can be fitted inside one of these. But actually, they're not actually in this computer here, they are in fact in another central one somewhere else.

GENGIS: How proud it makes me feel, to be alive at such an exciting time.

UNCLE: Everyone feels that. You see, every iota of human information ever known can be stored in here.

GENGIS: Marvellous.

UNCLE: It puts us into contact with other like-minded people to exchange facts and opinions.

GENGIS: Fantastic.

UNCLE: Want to try it?

GENGIS: May I?

UNCLE: Go ahead.

GENGIS walks up to it slowly and starts to have sexual intercourse with it, violently and passionately, ranging across the room in a wild embrace. The machine is completely destroyed, smashed to bits, but GENGIS is satisfied.

Pause.

GENGIS: Hmm. Not bad… Can you get me another one?

UNCLE: I'll try.

II

UNCLE: Gengis, we've got a problem. Profits are down.

GENGIS: Again? How come?

UNCLE: The machines get bigger – the profits get smaller.

GENGIS: I thought if we make enough of something it hardly costs anything at all?

UNCLE: The trouble is, how do you make so many people buy the same thing?

GENGIS: Hm, yes, the chances of fifty million people buying exactly the same thing are about twenty-five million to one.

UNCLE: Yes. What can we do?

GENGIS: We could…try to make all the *people* exactly the same.

UNCLE: Aha yes! Tailor the body to fit the suit, so to speak.

GENGIS: No, it will never work.

UNCLE: Ridiculous idea! We'd have to brainwash them!

GENGIS: Damn yes, it's impossible.

UNCLE: I'd have to give them…about, say, at a rough estimate, two minutes outright brainwashing every fifteen minutes all through the evening.

GENGIS: Luckily, there's no chance of that.

UNCLE: No. And I'd have to put up posters in the streets and I'd have to have the best artists, wordsmiths and performers, in fact the most persuasive people among them, to help me.

GENGIS: Not a hope.

UNCLE: And pay them enormous amounts to help them overcome the shame and embarrassment of lying to the others.

GENGIS: Only the old Soviet Russians could do anything like it. Those ridiculous posters and absurd unbelievable slogans! Ha ha! What a laugh! Luckily we don't live under a system like that.

UNCLE: Most fortunate.

GENGIS: It's lucky that our beloved Capitalism for example is the most natural way of responding to the people's needs –

UNCLE: Very lucky.

GENGIS: It's the people who decide what our priorities are.

UNCLE: Absolutely.

GENGIS: The people themselves. Each individual has a voice.

Pause.

Actually, just remind me; how do the people let the system know what they have decided?

UNCLE: Through demand.

GENGIS: Ah yes, supply and demand. The people demand and lo and behold – it appears on the shelves!

UNCLE: Em…well, no. Not quite. Nearly. But…well, the other way around.

GENGIS: The other way around?

UNCLE: Yes. The thing appears on the shelves, then the people demand it.

GENGIS: Ah, (*Pause.*) but, how do the manufacturers know the people need it?

UNCLE: They know because *they* decide what the people want.

GENGIS: Isn't that a bit like the Communist system?

UNCLE: Ah, no. Because here it's not what the people *need* that is important, but what they *want*.

GENGIS: Oh. I see. And, how do we know what the people want? Do they tell us?

UNCLE: No, we tell them.

GENGIS: We tell them?

UNCLE: That is we encourage them to want what is convenient for us to make.

GENGIS: That saves a lot of wasted shampoo, I guess?

UNCLE: Oceans of it.

III

GENGIS: Uncle, may I ask why the furniture is always covered up with white sheets?

UNCLE: That's because we've got the decorators in.

GENGIS: They've been in for the past fifteen years, what's going on?

UNCLE: Constant renewal.

GENGIS: I've never even *seen* the furniture.

UNCLE: What a pity. Several different three-piece suites have come and gone beneath the sheets, not to mention fifteen fitted kitchens, twenty-eight stereos, twelve carpets, eighty-three beds, seventeen thousand bathroom suites and three hundred and twenty-six mug trees.

GENGIS: Is that why there's always a pile of broken furniture outside in the street? You know, I think this room has been repainted so often it's shrinking.

UNCLE: Things *do* wear out quickly these days but don't worry, your Royal Acquisitiveness, it's all so that we can be sure enough profit is generated in the economy.

GENGIS: Oh good. I suppose that *is* good isn't it?

UNCLE: Oh yes, it's very good.

GENGIS: What do we…do…with it?

UNCLE: Well, it allows us to afford new carpets, beds, and bathrooms.

GENGIS: Yes, that's just as well. Because they wear out so...quickly.

UNCLE: Yes.

GENGIS thinks, is about to ask something.

AUNTY comes in dressed like cross between an Hawaiian dancer and a member of the Orange Order: grass skirt, Orange sash, and bowler hat.

GENGIS: Are you sure that is an appropriate costume for you as headmistress of a mondo-cultural, maxi-lingual, primary school for the kids whose parents weren't middle-class enough to pretend to be Christians to get them into the church schools?

AUNTY: Yes. It's my St Patrick's Day outfit.

GENGIS: And who are you?

AUNTY: I'm Mother Christmas – and here are your presents.

GENGIS: What is it?

AUNTY: A bottle of wine.

GENGIS: Lovely.

AUNTY: I've ordered a shamrock tree for Uncle though.

GENGIS: You're keeping a bit of the Irish flavour then?

IV

GENGIS: I'm bored already. This is worse than last time.

AUNTY: Why don't you look up some of your old friends and admirers.

GENGIS: Very funny.

UNCLE: You must try to get some new ones.

AUNTY: Yes, you must appeal to Youth.

GENGIS: Youth?

AUNTY: Ah yes, Youth.

UNCLE: That's right. Tomorrow's people for tomorrow's world.

GENGIS: What are you talking about?

AUNTY: Youth are today's people!

UNCLE: Yes, Youth! Today's people...!

GENGIS: What does that make us?

AUNTY: (*With a misplaced enthusiastic venom.*) Yesterday's people!

GENGIS: But young people are selfish narrow-minded bigots.

UNCLE: They'll grow out of it.

GENGIS: Exactly. Can't we wait until they do, and *then* admire them? When they're older.

AUNTY: But who else would buy all the...items we sell them?

GENGIS: That reminds me... It's nearly Christmas, only two hundred and fifty-two shopping days left. I'd like to give my people a really surprising present, but what do you give someone who has nearly everything? My people are spoilt.

UNCLE: Just give them more of the same but call it something else.

GENGIS: They're too used to that. (*He paces about thoughtfully.*) No, it has to be something really unusual, to keep them interested, otherwise they get that glassy look in their eyes and that just makes me wild. I've got it! I can take away what they already have.

UNCLE: Oh no that wouldn't be very Christmassy.

GENGIS: Wouldn't it? Alright, then I'll do it right now! Now what shall I take away from their luxurious homes, bearing in mind that we'll have to use it all up ourselves, we don't want to waste anything.

UNCLE: Em...em.

AUNTY: Em...em

UNCLE: Em...em

AUNTY: Em...em

UNCLE: Em...em

GENGIS: Come on what have they got, that we want?

UNCLE: ...Well

AUNTY: ...Well

UNCLE: ...Well

AUNTY: ...Well

UNCLE: Nothing comes to mind.

GENGIS: Nothing? What about their...TVs and videos?

UNCLE: Do we really want that stuff? None of us know how to use it.

GENGIS: Neither do they. Alright then, how about their coffee machines?

UNCLE: Their kettle?

GENGIS: Or their...you know, those things they play music on.

UNCLE: Their cars?

GENGIS: No, the em…

UNCLE: Drums?

GENGIS: No, you know…

UNCLE: Forget it Gengis, we don't know, we're too old.

AUNTY: Their furniture!

GENGIS: You're joking; fish boxes with draylon stapled to it?

AUNTY: What else is there?

UNCLE: Em.

AUNTY: Em.

GENGIS: Christ!

AUNTY: There must be something we've forgotten.

UNCLE: Nope, That's about it.

GENGIS: Blimey. Poor bastards. And this is what everything has been sacrificed for?

UNCLE: So it appears. They have less than ever.

GENGIS: So what was the last hundred and fifty years about then?

UNCLE: Making you rich, O great industrial potentate!

GENGIS: Right, but what's next?

UNCLE: Nothing really.

GENGIS: You mean that's it?

UNCLE: Unless you'd like some more?

GENGIS: I wouldn't say no but, …my people!

UNCLE: Don't worry, they have their rewards; their hair is some of the cleanest in the world.

AUNTY: And you can smell the cleanness in their clothes from a very long way off indeed.

UNCLE: They have your great cleanser factory to thank for that.

GENGIS: They're buying are they?

UNCLE: Yes. First they work very hard to produce…items, all day long, then, when their day is done, they rush to the shops to buy it all.

GENGIS: And in the evenings?

UNCLE: Who knows? Sick it all up I suppose, onto their sofas.

GENGIS: And yet despite all this, I still get the impression they are greedy emptyminded acquisitive scum. How is that?

UNCLE: They have a fierce attachment to what they haven't got.

GENGIS: This sounds like an idea that could catch on, global-wise. I suggest we leave the castle confines and spread the…whatever we have, all around the world.

UNCLE: Its been done already.

GENGIS: Has it?

UNCLE: Yes, every country is identical.

GENGIS: Surely there is something more we have to give to the world?

UNCLE: No.

GENGIS: Liberty and justice?

UNCLE laughs.

Oh 'ha ha ha'. Very easy. Alright, let's make that: T-shirts with *Liberty and Justice* written on them.

UNCLE: They make their own.

GENGIS: (*Horrified.*) They make their own?? We really are in the shit then.

V

Enter AUNTY dressed as a cross between Stalin and Mao-Tse-Tung

GENGIS: What's that you're wearing Aunty?

AUNTY: It's my Yam Festival outfit.

GENGIS: Oh, it looks more like a cross between Stalin and Mao-Tse-Tung.

AUNTY: No, it's Pol Pot actually.

GENGIS: It's very eye-catching. And what is the Yam Festival actually?

AUNTY: It's a kind of Harvest Festival.

GENGIS: Tins of beans, that kind of thing?

AUNTY: Yes.

GENGIS: And er...

AUNTY: Well, you don't think I'm going to represent Africans as superstitious primitives who still believe in the power of nature.

GENGIS: God forbid that anyone should be that primitive!

AUNTY: So, I'm going to emphasise the political nature of the production cycle, and show the year as a kind of four-season plan, with quotas and targets enforced with a rule of absolute terror.

GENGIS: That's much better.

AUNTY: Where there is nonsense we shall bring sense.

GENGIS: Well, Aunty. All I can say is, I'm really looking forward to Christmas.

AUNTY: Christmas? You mean Xmas, the season of Blandness and Greed? So am I.

GENGIS: I'm glad that Xmas at least is allowed to retain some of it's cultural identity.

AUNTY: We retain only the elements that can appeal to *everyone.*

GENGIS: Aunty, I have at last thought of something that most of our people haven't got.

AUNTY: Ooh Gengis, you're so innovative!

GENGIS: Yes. Here it is.

AUNTY: What is it?

GENGIS: A noose.

AUNTY: So chic. May I try it on?

GENGIS: You'll get your chance. We can make a fortune. Production costs will be low, and the price the suckers will pay will be high.

AUNTY: It's a great strategy. What will you call it?

GENGIS: The 'Money for Old Rope' strategy.

AUNTY: I'm stunned, Gengis. Excellent.

GENGIS: Give the people enough rope, and they will hang them*selves.*

AUNTY: How thrilling and chilling!

GENGIS: It's aimed chiefly at the young –

AUNTY: How refreshingly irresponsible. Teenagers will love it!

GENGIS: Yes. It's like gravity, just pull the lever and the mass will fall.

AUNTY: (*Excited.*) The mass will fall!

GENGIS: And you're quite right Aunty except in one thing: we shall not market this to teenagers.

AUNTY: We won't? How socially aware of you Gengis – I'm impressed.

GENGIS: Exactly. No, we shall aim at the *really* important consumer group, the *tween*agers, the seven- to twelve-year olds.

AUNTY: Aren't they a little young to be hanging themselves?

GENGIS: They grow up so quickly these days. The best way to sell this gear, I have decided, is to run a tweenzine…with a problems page.

AUNTY: But we have no letters.

GENGIS: We can write them ourselves, just to get the little dears started, so they know what to think.

AUNTY: You start then…

GENGIS: Dear Julie…

AUNTY: Dear Judy…

GENGIS: Dear Jude…

AUNTY: Dear Judas…

GENGIS: Dear Judas…my boyfriend says I ought to hang myself…but I think I might be too young. He is eighteen but I am only eight. Please help me. PS, my mum says I'm a little tart and that hanging's too good for me.

AUNTY: Dear young friend, I can tell that you are a lot more mature than those around you. Taking the initiative to write to me shows great wisdom beyond your years. I'd say you're more than ready to hang yourself. But change your boyfriend first.

GENGIS: Excellent advice. Dear Judas...everyone in my class has got a noose and they say I'm rubbish because I don't have one. Should I give in? Or should I stick up for myself. I am seven.

AUNTY: Stroppy little slag!

GENGIS: The reply Aunty!

AUNTY: Dear young person, It seems to me that it's time you woke up to the fact that there are more people in the world than just you. Get out there! Don't stay at home moping. Put on a new face, get yourself a makeover, put on a new pair of tights, and, yes, get a noose. Why not? It's okay to be strong-minded but you don't want to be a freak do you? Be yourself – get a noose, and join in the fun.

GENGIS: Well done Aunty.

AUNTY: Why can't parents and teachers be as streetwise as this Judas person?

GENGIS: It's you Aunty. Try this one: Dear Judas, my mum says nooses are for older girls and that I should be playing with dolls. I'm all confused. I'm already five years old.

AUNTY: Difficult one. Dear Anonymous, people develop at different ages. Your mum only wants what's best for you but if you don't get into the scene now people will laugh at you and call you names when you get older and you don't want that. But you must decide for yourself.

GENGIS: Good, Aunty.

AUNTY: What is the matter with these people?

GENGIS: Actually I don't like the word noose. It sounds so constricting. (*He fingers his collar nervously.*)

VI

GENGIS: Uncle, Uncle, the fairy lights and tinsel are up in the shops! It must be Christmas! O how I love Christmas!

UNCLE: It's October, Gengis.

GENGIS: Yes, yes. Christ I feel stressed. The trouble is, the real spirit has gone out of it. Still, the children like it. It's for the children isn't it?

UNCLE: Yes, Christmas is for the children.

GENGIS: Yes, Christmas is for the children.

UNCLE: Yes, it's for the children, the children like it.

GENGIS: Yes, Christmas is for the children.

UNCLE: Yes, Christmas is for the children.

GENGIS: Yes, Christmas is for the children.

UNCLE: Yes, Christmas is for the children.

GENGIS: Yes... Why is it for the children?

UNCLE: Because they get presents.

GENGIS: Spoilt little bastards. That greedy look in their eyes, already looking for the next present before they've even unwrapped the one in their filthy hands.

UNCLE: It used to be a spiritual time.

GENGIS: Yes the festival of the Divine Scapegoat.

UNCLE: Ah yes, God bless Him.

GENGIS: The world doesn't want any favours now eh Uncle? It doesn't need that pervert.

UNCLE: All homegrown superstition has been eradicated.

GENGIS: Shit. I had a really good idea just now, and I've forgotten it.

UNCLE: Oh go on, what was it?

GENGIS: No – it's gone right out of my head.

UNCLE: What was it to do with?

GENGIS: Leave it, Uncle.

UNCLE: Please.

GENGIS: I've got jam on my nose, how did that get there? Ow! Now I've wiped it into my eye!

UNCLE: What we need is someone to guide the royal spoon.

GENGIS: I have decided to use my position of great authority and influence to say just this one thing to the people in plain language: I want to replace the present economic system with something else based on peace love and understanding, and also common sense. I shall announce it.

UNCLE: Gengis no, it upsets people.

GENGIS: Don't they know what love is?

UNCLE: No they don't.

GENGIS: (*Sighs.*) Uncle, all this thinking has given me an erection. How about one of those computers of yours?

UNCLE: I could get you a calculator.

GENGIS: What kind of man do you think I am?

UNCLE: Alright, a widescreen TV with surround sound.

GENGIS: A what?? What on earth is that?

UNCLE: They're cheap but they won't rush you.

GENGIS: Yes, and you end up with spots on your dick.

UNCLE: Not if you're careful.

GENGIS: I don't want to be careful.

UNCLE: Alright, how about a garden chair?

GENGIS: Mmm. A garden chair...

UNCLE: Or a set.

GENGIS: Hmmm!!

UNCLE: Foldable. In white plastic.

GENGIS: (*Sniggers.*)

UNCLE: Floral design, with air freshener release button, fully charged.

GENGIS turns, walks away.

What is it?

GENGIS: (*Laughs a bit, embarrassed.*) Sorry Uncle. (*Turns back again towards UNCLE.*)

UNCLE: What? Urgh!

He looks at GENGIS's trousers and sees that GENGIS has come inside them. It is dripping.

GENGIS: I like this home shopping.

UNCLE: You need to get out and about.

GENGIS: (*Sits down, breathing heavily.*) I need a rest now. Leave me in my royal solitude.

UNCLE: Impossible I'm afraid. You see, your mobile phone is ringing.

GENGIS: Oh God, where is it now?

UNCLE: It's on the bus, ten minutes from home. It wants to tell you something but you must wait until it gets in.

GENGIS: Bloody marvellous. I need a rest.

A very loud 'click' is heard, followed by a Siberian wind.

What's that?

UNCLE: That was the Gulf Stream being turned off. You see, the sky is turning black and the rivers are rising. There's such a chill in the air, my goodness. Mittens on! Jump into your canoe! Either pollution has gone up or US tree oxygen production has slumped.

GENGIS: Look Uncle, I'll just take a stroll outside if you don't mind, down to get a fish paste chicken burger. It's so spicy, extra spicy, spicy, spicy, spicy, yum yum, tasty Mmm, hot flaming spicy chicken paste. Tastes like fucking porridge, I can't wait.

UNCLE: A brochooore has arrived, Your Exquisiteness, outlining your policy on…em…something or other.

GENGIS: My policy?

UNCLE: So it says.

GENGIS: Hmm. And er…how did it seem?

UNCLE: Very impressive indeed. More something for eight per cent of the under fives, and less something else for…someone else. And a lot of stuff about young people.

GENGIS: (*Unusually aggressive.*) O not again!! I hate young people! I'd like to open a special factory where youngsters can make their own clothes, you know, Bad Experience or whatever its called.

UNCLE: Work Experience.

GENGIS: That's it. A great big sweat-shop stitching on labels onto their blouses.

AUNTY: What about their human rights.

GENGIS: Not applicable.

AUNTY: O!

UNCLE: He's raving, Aunty. He's becoming intelligible, and when he's intelligible he's dull.

VII

GENGIS: Aunty there's someone screaming in the street.

AUNTY: It's an echo dear, an echo from the past.

GENGIS: Is it someone in distress do you think? Shall I go out and help?

AUNTY: Have you the time? Aren't you a hundred per cent busy with your lifestyle management?

GENGIS: It's by careful lifestyle management that I can have free time to help others. Listen do you hear that?

VOICE FROM THE STREET: Help, help! O Help please!

GENGIS: Perhaps its someone dying of loneliness or hunger?

AUNTY: Or even a bad career move or their house sale fell through.

GENGIS: Do you think so?

AUNTY: These are today's kinda problems, Gengis.

GENGIS: Alright, I'll ignore it then.

He starts doing something.

VOICE FROM THE STREET: Help help! O please somebody help me!

Long pause.

O help please!

Long pause.

Silence.

GENGIS: Do you like double glazing? I don't. It looks... like shit.

Pause.

And I like a draught. It's healthy.

AUNTY: Double glazing is very attractive, clean and neat. I like modern things, they're more better innit?

GENGIS: You know this profit business? I've been thinking; what's it for?

AUNTY: It's to pay for the hospitals and schools. Which is why it really doesn't matter how we generate the profit, its all in a good cause. However futile your purchase, you are doing good. There is no such thing as waste. Even my collection of twenty-five thousand fluffy toys is to good purpose. It actually pays for three hospitals and all the meals-on-wheels in Dagenham.

GENGIS: I knew you'd say that. And how does that work?

AUNTY: Through tax, little Gengis. A tax on the profit the nice man makes who grows my cuddly toys.

GENGIS: That's very good...except that tax on profits only accounts for twenty-five per cent of all revenues, the rest is income tax, and spending tax, both of which are a tax on labour, not profit.

AUNTY: Gengis, it's important not to bore the audience.

GENGIS: Alright then. Shall we have a little break?

UNCLE: Yes.

GENGIS: Okay.

UNCLE: What shall we do during the break, huh?

GENGIS: How about some cheap jokes aimed at easy targets? The Royal Family.

UNCLE: Hahahahahahaha.

GENGIS: The Pope.

UNCLE: Hahahahahahahaha.

GENGIS: English attempts at religion.

UNCLE: Hahahahahahahaha.

GENGIS: Morris Dancing.

UNCLE: Hahahahahahahaha.

GENGIS: Slightly old fashioned things.

UNCLE: Hahahahahahahahahahahahahaha.

GENGIS: The establishment – as it was in 1958, not the new one. (*He gestures indicating his immediate surroundings.*)

UNCLE: Hahahahahahahahahahahahahahahahahahaha.

GENGIS: Shutup.

UNCLE: By the way, since you mention it, the people are complaining about taxation, Your Royal Superficiality.

GENGIS: Are they now? I've been waiting for this. Well, let us see; who is complaining?

UNCLE: The very poor.

GENGIS: They don't pay any. Anyone else?

UNCLE: The poor.

GENGIS: They pay very little, and get a lot. Next?

UNCLE: The nearly poor.

GENGIS: The nearly poor are complaining? But without tax they would *be* poor, because they can't afford to pay for anything themselves.

UNCLE: They are in agreement sire, and are grateful for the schools and hospitals, but in view of the fact that their pay packet is so small they resent it being made even smaller.

GENGIS: Presumably this is a sensation they are well used to as they must feel it every time they spend any money. I'd like to see them spend it more wisely than the way I spend it for them. Tell them to sod off.

UNCLE: Yes, m'lud.

GENGIS: Anyone else?

UNCLE: The industrialists sire, and the middle classes: they all hate tax.

GENGIS: Alright then, abolish it.

UNCLE: Most wise sire. The pound in your pocket, we shall say to them, is safe at last. Trust us, the government of *no* taxation.

GENGIS: Yes abolish it. Every man for himself. No schools, no hospitals. Now let's see where the captains of industry find the thirty-eight billion it costs to teach their employees to read and write and frigg their computers, and the forty-three billion a year it costs to cure their broken bowels they get from being sodomised in the workplace, cure them so they are fit and ready for work and not wasting a load of man-hours.

UNCLE: Ah.

GENGIS: Suddenly tax is popular with industry once again.

UNCLE: What about the middle classes, my majesty, perhaps they feel they can afford the essential services themselves privately?

GENGIS: And yet, and yet, however bad we make the schools and hospitals, they will insist on using them won't they? It's funny really.

UNCLE: Yes, it's funny really.

GENGIS: And in fact they're the ones who want them to be better.

UNCLE: Ha ha yes!

GENGIS: So they'd better fucking pay for it.

UNCLE: Let them pay. No, no-one gives anything for free.

GENGIS: No-one so much as picks up a piece of paper and puts it in the bin. Talking of bins, I'd like you to meet someone from my part of town.

He ushers in ANNIE.

UNCLE: What a remarkably attractive young lady. May I enquire the whereabouts of your personal residence?

ANNIE: Finsbury Park.

UNCLE: How swish. I have many a time visited the pleasure gardens there.

ANNIE: I'm a nurse, actually.

UNCLE: Ah… I seem to recall… You ring a very lovely bell. I've heard a lot about you

GENGIS: Now, stand there Uncle, I'd like to illustrate something.

UNCLE: Illustrate away my boy.

GENGIS: Now, let's say there are four people in this economy. Annie, who is a nurse and takes care of our...wellbeing; myself, a farmer who provides the meat for beef sandwiches for Annie and the rest of us; Aunty, who provides the slices of bread between which the beef is inserted; and then there's Uncle who manufactures cuddly toys.

UNCLE: What kind?

GENGIS: Soft pink pussies, they are Aunty's special predilection.

UNCLE: Okay.

GENGIS: Now –

UNCLE: May I ask a question?

GENGIS: Yes, alright

UNCLE: Do I provide an aftersales customer care pussy servicing service?

GENGIS: Well, I suppose...

UNCLE: I think it's only right in the circumstances.

GENGIS: Okay. Now, the question is, which one's labour can society do without? Which one, for example, is providing the health care? Is it Uncle? Or is it Annie?

UNCLE: I would say that it is very obviously Annie who provides that most valuable commodity.

GENGIS: Thank you Uncle. It isn't you then? You aren't paying for it in some way?

UNCLE: No, for I am making cuddly toys, though no doubt I am supplying them to all and sundry, not just Aunty, for example but also, to Annie here?

GENGIS: Quite likely. Now whose labour can we dispense with? Mine and Aunty's, who provide the beef sandwiches we all live on, or Uncle with his cuddly toys.

UNCLE: Excuse me a minute, but it depends doesn't it, Gengis on what kind of society we want. I mean, it's not always quite so clear-cut. Perhaps, now please excuse me dear lady if I take the liberty of saying so, perhaps Annie here would, on some occasions chose to go without a beef sandwich if she needs to get her pink pussy serviced; and that would mean more work for me and unemployment for you. Forgive my presumption.

ANNIE: Not at all, I'm sure.

AUNTY: Well, I don't know about this at all. I only want a nurse when I'm ill. The rest of the time, my priority is to have my pink pussies serviced properly.

UNCLE: Come now...

GENGIS: There should only be nurses when Aunty is ill; the rest of the time they may be employed working for Uncle perhaps?

UNCLE: Alongside me eh? Well, why not? If you have no objections my dear?

ANNIE: None at all, I'm sure.

GENGIS: Yes, but let us say, let us say there is a virulent pox going about, and we all need health-care. It is perhaps time for Uncle to go and work alongside Annie. But there is a conflict of interests.

UNCLE: How could there be?

GENGIS: Because, Uncle, although everyone has already purchased one of your cuddly toys, you have put up signs saying, 'Every good parent buys at least five cuddly toys for their child.'

UNCLE: A good move on my part, if I may say so. Otherwise I would be redundant.

GENGIS: Yes, a good move because otherwise it might seem to be better for parents to make sure there is health-care for their children to stave off the pox. But in fact the little signs work very well and everyone believes that what you say is true. No-one wants to be seen as an unloving parent, and so Annie is sent to work half-time for Uncle, so now there's not enough health-care. Not only that, but Uncle is rewarded by being given a bigger house than anyone else, a big car and all the beef sandwiches he can eat so that he becomes fat, while others go hungry. And to cap it all we say not just that Uncle is paying for the health-care, and that without him there wouldn't be any at all, but that somehow without him there wouldn't be *anything* at all and everything would collapse.

AUNTY: I don't see what the matter is. I would be willing to pay a premium for prompt servicing.

ANNIE: Wouldn't we all.

UNCLE: Come, come.

VIII

GENGIS: You know my people, surprisingly, don't seem to have any possessions. Why is that?

UNCLE: Because we don't sell them any.

GENGIS: But they do nothing else than buy things.

UNCLE: No, not strictly speaking, not things as such. More like nothings, but with the names of things written on them. It's the name they're buying.

GENGIS: But where are all the nothings...there must be a tremendous amount of them...lying around?

UNCLE: No. We have designed the nothings to self-destruct over only a few weeks, leaving plenty of space for the purchase of new nothings to replace them.

GENGIS: And yet there seems remarkably little space left.

UNCLE: Yes, there is the small matter of the debris. Oh yes, we scatter the debris far and wide, as close to Nigeria as we can get. It's a global solution for a global planet.

GENGIS: Hadn't we better make fewer nothings to save the little space that's left?

UNCLE: No, *au contraire*, we must accelerate production output of nothings; it's a matter of some urgency.

GENGIS: A matter of urgency? Why is that?

UNCLE: Because the materials are running out.

GENGIS: Materials? To make nothings? Surely not?

UNCLE: Oh yes, one uses an awful lot of materials, and they're running out fast.

GENGIS: Are they?

UNCLE: Yes, it will be all gone by August 2038 to be precise. So there's no time to lose. Growth is what we need, no question of it.

GENGIS: No, no question of that.

UNCLE: Growth, growth, growth.

GENGIS: Yes! yes! yes! We don't want the economy to shrink do we?

UNCLE: (*Screams.*) The very thought!

GENGIS: Let's agree never to discuss it again.

UNCLE: Not for one single second will we consider whether growth is a good thing.

GENGIS: Never, not until eternal blackness shall cover the earth and mankind is extinct.

UNCLE: Serve him right.

GENGIS: What a cunt.

UNCLE: Yep.

IX

GENGIS: Uncle, …aren't the people a little sad having all these nothings?

UNCLE: It serves them right for being so materialistic; we are trying to make them more spiritual.

GENGIS: Oh I'm moved.

UNCLE: To find fulfilment…

GENGIS: Fulfilment is just what they need.

UNCLE: And a brand new sense of morality.

GENGIS: Marvellous. And when do they get this brand new sense of moral and spiritual fulfilment?

UNCLE: When they go shopping.

GENGIS: Hm…convenient.

UNCLE: Yes.

GENGIS: Convenient because parking is already provided.

UNCLE: Exactly. And so although they *seem* to be leaving the superhypermegamarket with Espace loads of sugar, salt, coloured water and breakables and unendurables, in fact, when the happy-clean kids unload the boot in the

paved driveway they are unloading aspirations of a
personal nature.

GENGIS: You don't say. Not *too* personal I hope?

UNCLE: No, it's families, it's clean, it's kids, it's hip, it's
hop, it's a way of life. It's what and who they want to be.

GENGIS: And er, …they unload this from the car boot?

UNCLE: Yes. Then they take the sugar and salt and inject it
directly into their children.

GENGIS: You mean they jack up?

UNCLE: Yes.

GENGIS: Neat. And the kids become spiritual in this way?

UNCLE: Yes. Then they dress their kids up in clothes made
by poor little fingers of other kids all around the globe
of all colours; its a human rainbow. And we've told them
that when you piss on someone, a rainbow forms, and
when you see a rainbow you must make a wish; and in
that wish you must include the hope that all the little
rainbow children can one day be just like you, and go
shopping in a big car with Marmie and Daaddy, and
dargie and not be dirty and poor and human shite no
more, because we lurv them, we looourv them so so so
much that we shhshshshshop them, their little brown
bodies, until we take them home with us and eat them;
and our wish is fulfilled each time we wish for an item of
clothes, or an IT system, or a business solution, or a
cookie, or a snookie, or drink a cup of caaaffee in the
Starfucker caaaffee house on the block.

GENGIS: Well, I'm relieved to hear it, Uncle. I was
worried, you know, about the way things are going.

UNCLE: Yes we were all worried. There's so much to worry
about.

GENGIS: I was getting worry overload, as they say. I was worried that –

UNCLE: Say no more. Don't worry.

GENGIS: Uncle do you have a franchise in a brand of coffee called Rainbow or something like that, you keep going on about rainbows and coffee?

UNCLE: Rainbows and coffee aren't just words, Gengis, they're a way of life – they're a way of death too, and everything in between.

GENGIS: Can I buy this somewhere?

UNCLE: No purchase necessary. At Rainbow Coffee we don't want you to buy our product like other companies do, we don't ask from anyone, more than they can manage; for some of us it means taking a break from our busy lives and taking quality time with a cup of Rainbow coffee, or just drop in at one of our resting centres to meditate and chill with likemindeds over a frothing Cap o' Chino. And, hey. If that's all you can manage, that's cool. So long as when you face your god at the end of it all you can say: I did this, or that, what did you do? Krishna Murti, or Jesus, or Aslan the Invincible, or Jehova, or Mr Islam? Because there are folks, real brothers of the rainbow, who sleep, eat and live coffee; they pick it, melt it down, pack it into vacuum-packed-for-freshness packs, just for you. That's the message they're sending you. Whatever you want to make of it, that's up to you. And then in th' evenin', when their working day is done, they relax and smile at the brown coffee sun, and just dream...dream of a better world, a rainbow world, and we just ask you to share that dream, just for one minute every day. Is that too much to ask? I don't know.

GENGIS: So what you're saying Uncle, is that you want people to drink your brand of coffee?

UNCLE: Yes.

GENGIS: I think I prefer tea.

End of Part One.

PART TWO

X

GENGIS: It's no good, I've had enough, I'm going to rebel; I'm going to make it my mission to try to persuade everyone in the world not to be so greedy and stupid, and to make do with what they've got, and be loving and peaceful to all men. How's that?

UNCLE: Well, good luck, Gengis.

AUNTY: Yes, good luck.

UNCLE: Yes. (*Shakes his hand.*) Well done old boy.

AUNTY: Yes. Well done, Gengis, very nice of you…

UNCLE: Let us know how you get on.

AUNTY: Send us a fax, or mail us an e.

UNCLE: e-mail us.

AUNTY: Yes, e-mail us a fax. Send us some surf.

GENGIS: I see. And what are you two going to do?

AUNTY: We'll stay and guard the fort…

UNCLE: Yes, don't mind us.

AUNTY: We've got some key purchases to make.

UNCLE: And the hoovering…

AUNTY: Yes, there's the hoovering to do.

GENGIS: Hm… I feel as if you despise my new-found kind and loving nature, you seem too busy to talk to me.

AUNTY: Ah yes Gengis; but that's the main difficulty you're going to have.

UNCLE: Yes, people will be doing this all the time.

GENGIS: Will they now?

AUNTY: Yes, that's why we're not kind and loving too.

UNCLE: Otherwise we would be, wouldn't we?

AUNTY: Oh yes, of course we would. And deep down we really are...

UNCLE: Oh yes, we really really are. But the world, you see Gengis, is not loving and giving.

AUNTY: So we have to be prepared, for example, to be a little reserved sometimes, a little, just a little, less than over-generous...

UNCLE: A little cool with people sometimes.

AUNTY: Yes, a little cool, or *un peu froid.*

UNCLE: You sometimes just have to put yourself and your family first before you go around helping all and sundry.

AUNTY: Yes, sometimes, because of the way the world is, you have to say: Sorry chum, I just can't help you today, I have a family to feed...

UNCLE: Yes, exactly. Charity starts at home.

AUNTY: Yes, and sometimes you have to say: Please don't pester me, I'm a woman.

UNCLE: Or a man.

AUNTY: Or a man, and I'm walking home, on my own. And sometimes because of the way the world is, you have to say: So that's your little game is it? Just you wait!

UNCLE: Some people, Gengis, are low, they'll stop at nothing.

AUNTY: Yes, they only care about number one.

UNCLE: It's dog eat dog out there, Gengis lad.

AUNTY: You have to watch your back all the time, it's tooth and claw. You just can't give these people a basket of fruit and hope they'll go away politely, they won't.

UNCLE: Sometimes you have to say: Listen mate, what's your fucking problem?

AUNTY: They want your job. They're armed. They'll stop at nothing.

UNCLE: Sometimes you have to say: Do you want some? Eh? Eh? Come on then!! Come on!!

AUNTY: Yes, and you have to be willing, Gengis, to put the boot in good and hard, right in the testicles and keep it there until all their children are dead.

Silence.

Long pause.

GENGIS: Alright, I'll go on my own then.

UNCLE: Sometimes, Gengis, military action is unavoidable. Sometimes they slaughter innocent men, women and children. What can you do in the face of that?

GENGIS: I don't know. What can you do?

UNCLE: You can slaughter innocent men women and children back again in response.

AUNTY: Yes, it's just a matter of remembering who did it first.

XI

GENGIS: Uncle, I've for a long time now been attracted to the idea of crawling along the pavement on my hands and knees. Would you care to come out and join me?

UNCLE: No thank you, Gengis, the skin at the front of my knees won't bend in that direction. Where does this impulse come from?

GENGIS: It comes from being very tired.

UNCLE: Gengis, perhaps I should take this opportunity of telling you some rather bad news.

GENGIS: O yes? Do go on.

UNCLE: You are no longer king.

GENGIS: Aren't I? I thought this was coming. What am I then?

UNCLE: You're a kind of...relic. A reminder of what things used to be, a piece of nostalgia, a warning to future generations, a person who sits in rooms having the same conversation over and over again, a freak, a failure, a man who walks along shouting in the street and arguing in supermarkets, a rag and bone man, a snob, a Luddite, an impediment, a bore, a pang of conscience, the lute the lyre, English folk music, dead, buried, forgotten, not regretted, not on the syllabus, not a target language, not a key scene, not a key skill, not on the fast track, not on prozac, you're not up, you're not in the magazine, you're not in the quiz, you don't wash, you're what we all want to avoid, the worry we don't need to have, the pig in the poke, the local library, the man in the corner, the girl by the wall, the privet hedge, the iron window frame, bold Mercutio, the grave man, an embarrassing erection, an epileptic, a pain in the arse, a piece of shit.

GENGIS: Who is king then?

UNCLE: The office of king has been abolished.

GENGIS: How nice. What have you got instead?

UNCLE: A kind of…manager.

GENGIS: Good is he?

UNCLE: We hardly notice him.

GENGIS slips from his chair. We share in his…blackout.

XII

AUNTY: Feeling better now Gengis?

GENGIS: What happened?

UNCLE: You fainted and made a mess on the floor.

GENGIS: Don't start hoping, it can happen to anyone.

AUNTY: Of course it can Gengis.

GENGIS: And now I'm feeling extra business-like and ready for some really demanding reforming work.

AUNTY: Super, shall I take notes?

GENGIS: Absolutely not. That's where the trouble begins, as I shall explain. No, you shall remember what I say, and if you can't remember it, forget it.

AUNTY: Okay, I'm all ready.

GENGIS: Alright. Step one is to liberate language from the grips of the enemy; I shall abolish jargon.

AUNTY: …

GENGIS: Did you hear what I said? Why have you got that silly look on your face?

AUNTY: I haven't.

GENGIS: You did hear didn't you?

AUNTY: Yes.

GENGIS: Repeat it.

AUNTY: You shall abolish…something.

GENGIS: Jargon.

AUNTY: Yes.

GENGIS: Say it.

AUNTY: Abolish.

GENGIS: Jargon.

AUNTY: Mm.

GENGIS: Abolish –

AUNTY: It.

GENGIS: Abolish jargon.

AUNTY: Hurrah.

GENGIS: Aunty!

AUNTY: What?

GENGIS: If you don't say it I'll do something very unpleasant to your underwear.

AUNTY: Abolish jubblewabble.

GENGIS: Say it!

AUNTY: Abolish it.

GENGIS: Euphemisms.

AUNTY: Obernisms.

GENGIS: Lies.

AUNTY: Lines. Lobes. Looms. Abolish it.

GENGIS: We may have some difficulty with this one.

AUNTY: I'm ready.

GENGIS: This nation can be great again. It can rise out of the self-inflicted humiliation and speak the truth, Aunty. What do you think?

AUNTY clears her throat.

Aunty?

AUNTY's dry throat develops into a terrible choking, until finally she is strangled by her maidenhead, and falls for dead on the floor with her bloomers about her neck.

Maybe not.

She lies there, barely gasping.

You ought to develop your listening skills

Enter UNCLE.

UNCLE: What have you done to your aunty, boy?

GENGIS: I've accessed her excitability whatnot.

UNCLE: It looks more like you have strangled her with her knickers.

GENGIS: She met that particular challenge herself.

UNCLE: Is she dead?

GENGIS: She's certainly at one of her key stages of development.

UNCLE: My, my this is a turn up. How will this impact on the excellence 4 everyone program? [*sic.*]

GENGIS: You mean Aunty's ambitious scheme to take education into the new blah blah blah by giving an intense programme of enforced mediocrity to all the stupid, lazy, inattentive, bored, boring, rude, vulgar worthless, loudmouthed rubbish, the scum of the whole of Europe?

UNCLE: You're not very well boy, calm down. Help me try to release the gusset from her gullet.

GENGIS: Follow me into exile Uncle… I can't bear this anymore.

UNCLE: Alright, but let's really live it up before you go, let's really put ourselves where the knife cuts, where the truth hurts, where the walls come tumbling down on lies and hypocrisy, where small-minded complacency is put to ignominious flight, where the degradation and poison of marketing and consumerism is rejected flat and outright, where the pusillanimous daren't set foot, where the uncomfortable and difficult word is spoken regardless of the consequences, where wit and humour scoff at fear.

GENGIS: Let's go to *THE THEATRE!*

UNCLE: The Restaurant.

GENGIS: Yes, that's what I meant.

XIII

GENGIS: Aunty, I've invented something.

AUNTY: Thrills! What is it?

GENGIS: A television.

AUNTY: That's not new.

GENGIS: This one is soft and you can sit on it.

AUNTY: That's not a television.

GENGIS: What is it then?

AUNTY: A bottom.

GENGIS: A bottom. Talking of bottoms, would you excuse me for one moment, Aunty, I have some guests arriving.

GENGIS walks off stage and we hear him talking to what sounds like a very large crowd of people indeed.

(*Off.*) How dare you Sir! Step back! That's better. Mm. Fresh air at last. Could you all breathe *in* please? In…out. Make room there please! What I need is an office of my own. Move along there please! There's plenty of space up the back.

UNCLE comes in looking as if he has been somewhat pushed and shoved.

AUNTY: What is that terrible noise?

UNCLE: Someone told him you could get the whole population of the world standing shoulder to shoulder on the Isle of Wight.

GENGIS: (*Off.*) No, there's nowhere for you to park your boat, I'm afraid. Needles this way, Cowes the other…

AUNTY: Has he…?

UNCLE: Invited them all here at once? Yes.

AUNTY: What's that funny smell?

UNCLE: No idea… Wait now, wait; they're settling down.

AUNTY: They do fidget don't they!

A hum offstage halts.

GENGIS: (*Off.*) There. Now I've asked you all here today, to say but these few words: 'I hope we can all remain close when all this is over. Let pain and suffering be a thing of the past. Let's try and be nice to each other and share and share alike.' And now ladies and gentlemen.

Of course it's not easy to organise an event such as this, and er…as we know Cleanliness Is Part Of Our Everyday LifeStyle; tell your friends. And so we're very grateful to have on board, sponsoring the whole thing, Anal-Bright – without whom none of this would have been possible; Anal-Bright – for a cleaner tomorrow; tell your friends. And now a word from our sponsor:

UNCLE: This is me, Aunty.

AUNTY: Are *you* Anal-Bright?

UNCLE: I'm on the board so to speak, yes.

AUNTY: So it was you told him –

UNCLE: Shsh now Aunty: My speech! Step aside please!

Exit.

(*Off.*) Hi you guys! Is everybody having a good time! Now, who these days can distinguish between freedom of movement, even bowel movement, and freedom itself. That's what I'm here to say: I want Everybody to be free, every man woman and child. That's why we're starting a programme to supply bowel regulation packs to every household in the world by the year 2010. God be praised. Anal-Bright – putting science right back where it belongs…

Sound fades.

GENGIS comes in, pleased with himself.

GENGIS: What are you reading Aunty?

AUNTY: The tv mag.

GENGIS: (*Over her shoulder.*) And who are those lovely savoury looking people so smart and clean and casual roguish relaxed and clean and fit on the front page smiling so big and clean?

AUNTY: It's the Herring Family. 'How appearing on TV's *Hanging by the Neck Until You are Dead* changed our lives and those of our children.'

GENGIS: Hm, nice looking kids. A bit blue-lipped.

The sound of UNCLE's speech to the peoples of the world fades up again from offstage.

UNCLE: (*Off.*) ...and while you're all here, I've something very exciting to tell you: we're getting rid of those old fashioned Imperio-Christianical days of the week with its socio-hierarchical sabbathitical strictures in-built, with its stop-go, start-stop, enforced inactivity high wastage idle time, or 'weekend' as it used to be known in Victorian times – and replacing it with a new, fresh It's-your-life, Anal-Bright thirty-day decimal modern Life-unit; designer-made for today's busy people. No more will your life-shape be interrupted when *they* say every six days! Instead you'll be able to do what *you* want when *you* want to do it – leaving you free to make your own choices, meet friends, go out for a meal, or just relax in front of the TV! Life-Units, for today's kinda people.

GENGIS: It seems Uncle is short of man-hours to generate his shrinking profits.

AUNTY: That's right dearie; and they're ever so lazy and just want to rest rest rest and go fishing in the afternoons, like Karl Marx.

GENGIS: How dreary.

AUNTY: What we need is a bit of razzmatazz.

GENGIS: Alright, bring on the Americans.

Enter MAURICE PORKER.

GENGIS: Who are you? Don't you knock?

MAURICE: I am Maurice Porker.

GENGIS: Well, well, well.

MAURICE: I'm an American.

GENGIS: Are you? But you haven't got an accent.

MAURICE: What?

GENGIS: You know, Wah wah wah!

MAURICE: What's that supposed to be? Can we get down to business?

GENGIS: Oho business! I ought to have guessed! Oh yes! Ha ha.

MAURICE: I'm investigating for the House un-Appetising activities commission.

GENGIS: Mmm. And what are you looking for, mainly?

MAURICE: Anything un-American, anything we can't eat. You're a suspect.

GENGIS: Well, I'm not American, it's true.

MAURICE: No, Haha. We've noticed. And we've noticed how not much of what you do is in America's interests.

GENGIS: No, well, I'm sorry about that.

MAURICE: We hear you don't like American films, American slave bananas or the pyramid-shaped people we send to be tourists.

GENGIS: Nope. Nope. Nor the way you guzzle everyone else's food and other valuable resources and pollute the moon and stars and dirty the oceans in other people's backyards and enslave whole nations, nay, whole continents, all so you can get that pyramid shape. But don't worry Maurice, everything will be alright.

MAURICE: No, it won't. It won't be alright until you stop…

GENGIS: Stop what?

MAURICE: Stop doing things we find unappealing.

GENGIS: Maurice, Maurice, come here, that's it, come here. Now, Maurice. You're getting on my nerves. Now. Do you want a trade war?

MAURICE: That's what I came to threaten you with.

GENGIS: I thought so. It had to happen. Well just try me; Make my day.

MAURICE: I'll tell the chief pig.

GENGIS: Tell him.

MAURICE: So be it.

GENGIS: Up yours.

MAURICE: God is on our side!

GENGIS: Viva…Espagna!

MAURICE: Dollars!

GENGIS: Ex-colonial fairer-wage bananas, woollens. Films without explosions!

MAURICE: Disneyland!

GENGIS: The local library!

MAURICE: Disneyland Paris.

GENGIS: 'Paris Texas'.

Exit MAURICE.

Oh shit…

AUNTY: You've done it now Gengis.

GENGIS: I'm not anti-American, I just…

AUNTY: It's too late now.

GENGIS: At least we don't have to suck up to them anymore. At least we're doing what's right.

AUNTY: Does this mean we can say bad things about their foreign policy on the news?

GENGIS: Better check first. (*On the phone.*) Hello, Wally, this is the BBC here. Now we're having a trade war with the US, can we say bad things – ? He says: no we can't, in case we lose.

VOICE: (*From the street.*) Help me O please will nobody help me? Oh my God! Help me, help me for pity's sake!!

GENGIS: Ignore it Aunty, ignore it.

AUNTY: I was ignoring it.

GENGIS: No you weren't. It's affecting your breathing. I can hear your maidenhead squeaking from here. You're like an old accordion.

AUNTY: Sorry Gengis.

XIV

GENGIS: How do we fight a trade war, Uncle?

UNCLE: I've no idea.

GENGIS: We'll sell them more than they can possibly consume.

UNCLE: But the Americans claim to be able to consume the whole planet without even burping.

GENGIS: Burping? Burping? When I've finished with them they'll be, they'll be…farting! My sales drive will fill their gullets so quick they'll be blowing off right out of their damned cakeholes.

AUNTY: I don't think this trade war sounds altogether pleasant. It makes me nervous and scared. If you'll excuse me I'm going to the restroom.

UNCLE: What will you do there?

AUNTY: Whistle.

XV

UNCLE: Gengis, there's a chap outside says he's keen to join in the struggle against capitalism.

GENGIS: Exciting! Drag him in.

UNCLE: He seems to be wearing a disguise.

GENGIS: Is he a poor downtrodden type?

UNCLE: Ne, he's a billionaire.

GENGIS: I might have guessed.

UNCLE: I have his secret name written down here on a secret piece of paper.

UNCLE brings in the visitor, who wears a Nike T-shirt.

GENGIS: Ah, Mr…Whereyabinhidin'. Am I pronouncing that correctly?

WHEREYABINHIDIN': (*Silence.*)

GENGIS: So, well…you can take off that false beard now if you like, or would you like to remain inconspicuous?

WHEREYABINHIDIN': (*Silence.*)

GENGIS: Now, Mr Whereyabinhidin', what's your plan? Shall we liberate the downtrodden for example?

WHEREYABINHIDIN': (*Silence.*)

GENGIS: Shall we…feed the hungry? Some of your money might come in handy there… Mine is a bit tied-up you understand, in investments.

WHEREYABINHIDIN': (*Silence.*)

GENGIS: Yours is too? You don't say. Oh. Do tell. Now, let me guess. Where is your money invested? Texas? Very shrewd. I bought a retractable birdbath from there; would you like to see it? Oh? I see. Not the home improvements discount store? The oil fields! Oh yes. Yes, they do make 'em raw down there! I see. You don't say. All your money's invested in big American international companies and always has been since the 1970s. Terrific. Well, Mr Whereyabinhidin', its been wonderful to meet you…do call again –

WHEREYABINHIDIN': (*Silence. Gets up.*)

GENGIS: But, before you go…you haven't told me your plan yet. What means shall we employ to bring about happiness and freedom and spirituality in God's Garden?

WHEREYABINHIDIN': (*Whispers something to GENGIS.*)

GENGIS: Hmm. Well, thanks, but no thanks. Don't forget to pick up your hat on the way out.

WHEREYABINHIDIN' exits.

GENGIS watches him from the window. Sounds of a big American car and of screaming laughing beach boys and girls in the back as it drives off.

Hmm, …nice Cadillac. Pink.

UNCLE: Gee, he drives it like a natural, like a real redneck. Look at that baby go. Wooowee!

GENGIS: Some things you just can't hide, no matter how big your beard is.

AUNTY: Oh no! Look, some kiddies crossing the road. He'll never stop in time! He'll have to swerve into that tree!

UNCLE: His fenders will be ruined!!!

AUNTY: Oh, no, its alright. He went right over them.

UNCLE: Great suspension. Boing! Boing!

XVI

A heavy bombardment of high-tech missiles.

UNCLE: (*Comes in.*) What are you doing Gengis?

GENGIS: (*From under the table.*) I'm enduring freedom.

UNCLE: Yes, it can be arduous at times.

GENGIS: I thought this was meant to be a *trade* war?

UNCLE: Yes, I think this must be the bit to do with the arms trade.

GENGIS: I don't understand. What shall we do?

UNCLE: We could do what the other bombees do.

GENGIS: What's that?

UNCLE: Pretend to be winning until the country is smashed to bits – and then surrender.

An explosion.

GENGIS: Wow! I'm glad they can get pin-point accuracy with those things – that nearly missed!

Another explosion.

Tell me, Uncle, do you enjoy the live event or do you prefer to watch at home with a few beers?

Another explosion.

Start knitting a white flag, Aunty.

AUNTY: (*From where she crouches concealed beneath a piece of furniture.*) We have no white linen.

GENGIS: Use your bloomers.

AUNTY: They're not...white anymore.

GENGIS: Oh dear. Then hoist the brown flag.

AUNTY: (*Emerging from her hiding place.*) Alright.

AUNTY emerges wearing a Wonderwoman costume; Stars and Stripes knickers etc.

GENGIS: What's that you're wearing Aunty?

AUNTY: It's my Divali outfit. I'm on my way to school. As headmistress I'm setting an example in mult-eye culturalism.

GENGIS: Oh, it looks more like a Superwoman costume.

AUNTY: Oh I know; it's the thought that counts.

GENGIS: And what is the thought exactly, Aunty?

UNCLE: It's Maurice Porker, the US Ambassador, at the door. (*Rhymes.*)

GENGIS: Ah Maurice, Maurice, what can I do for you? Do sit down. (*He clears away some rubble for him.*) Sorry there are no luxurious cushions. You may squat on Aunty's face, if you don't mind the protruding nose and teeth; for you see, she is an English rose.

MAURICE: I've come to see if you guys want to give in yet. Have you had enough?

GENGIS: It's not as simple as all that Maurice. You see, this is a trade war, and we don't really feel as if we've done much trading yet. We've still got a few special offers we'd like to try out.

MAURICE: Oh yeah? Well, in your own time.

UNCLE: Gengis, a word. (*Aside.*) I thought you were going to surrender?

GENGIS: I know, I know. I'm sorry but the sight of Maurice has a funny effect on my temper.

MAURICE: You jerks don't even know what a trade war is do you? Ha ha ha!

GENGIS: You see what I mean? (*To MAURICE.*) Be with you in just a little moment Maurice.

UNCLE: But he's right. We don't know what a trade war is.

GENGIS: (*To MAURICE.*) Alright Maurice, how about you just *telling* us. We'd really rather you didn't stand there smirking, you see?

MAURICE: (*Big smile.*) Why sure!

GENGIS: Go on then.

MAURICE: A trade war starts when trade isn't carried out exactly as *we* want it, in a way that favours us and only us. Then…America, with her vast population, closes herself to your poxy little exports, like…well I don't know, Sherlock Holmes hats for example, or er, …er, I guess that's it. Anyway, we just stop buying them and you, er do the same back to us. We don't notice because the UK is so tiddly and we can sell our shit elsewhere, man, because the whole world is gagging for it, whereas I don't know where you gonna sell them Sherlock Holmes hats to as many suckers as *we* can supply. There just ain't that many suckers with cash anyplace else.

GENGIS: (*Visibly relieved.*) Ha ha! I can't believe it! Can this be true, Uncle? Maurice, you're pulling my leg aren't you? You mean we can ban American imports? Ha ha! You're joking. What bliss!! The nightmare is over! Just when it seemed it was too late for civilisation! We're free at last! Ha ha ha!

MAURICE: Is he crazy?

UNCLE: A little whimsical at times.

MAURICE: A little what? You guys had better get your shit together, y'know.

UNCLE: We will get our shit together...presently.

GENGIS: Uncle, I can't believe it, I'm so happy. Maurice, let me thank you. Let me...kiss you on the mouth.

MAURICE: Cool it y'homo.

GENGIS: The doom of inevitability has been lifted; just when I thought all of our children were going to be Americans, suddenly the future has returned to us after being away for so long.

XVII

GENGIS: Uncle, I've noticed we're not winning this trade war. We've got to hit them where they're vulnerable – intelligence work.

UNCLE: Most heroic, O great one. Neat.

GENGIS: I've decided to go undercover and research the US industrial base by taking a job in a US factory.

UNCLE: Industrial espionage. How exciting.

GENGIS: Take me there then. Take me to a factory at once.

UNCLE: Unfortunately I cannot do that.

GENGIS: Why not?

UNCLE: There are none. Not as such.

GENGIS: Not as such? No US factories as such? But where do they make all the carefully stitched, handwoven individually handmade and styled to the highest specification and styled and fashioned leesure wear that we'd all kill for? And all the soft drives for my hard top mobile?

UNCLE: In the Philippines.

GENGIS: I didn't know the Philippines was in America?

UNCLE: It isn't. America is in the Philippines. So is Britain. We have a finger in every pie.

GENGIS: Sounds like the perfect place for a working holiday.

UNCLE: Alright, if you insist. Here is your ticket, Let's Go Jiggy Jiggy Bucket Airticket, and here is mine, Corporate class, golf course on the top deck, in-flight brothel cum crèche on the lower deck. I love travel. Aunty will prepare your lunch box.

GENGIS: That's nice of her. Will I see you there?

UNCLE: Maybe. I have other business to attend to. I'm going on a tax holiday.

XVIII

GENGIS: Now, Aunty, about my disguise. I've tried to look like a Philippino. How is it?

AUNTY: No, it's all wrong.

GENGIS: What do they look like then?

AUNTY: Hard to say. The main thing is you've got the wrong sex; you must be a girlie.

GENGIS: A girlie?

AUNTY: Now, there are thirty million girlies from around the world to chose from; here are the pictures.

GENGIS: Hmm, nice. I recognise half of them from my Starving Babes Gallery on my floppy hard-on mobile disc gallery of babes.com.

AUNTY: That was before this employment opportunity came along. They all work here now. Right would you care to proceed to your accommodation?

GENGIS: Surely you don't work here? Perhaps you are an undercover agent like myself?

AUNTY: That's right, Gengis.

GENGIS: Where are we going? What is that awful smell?

AUNTY: It's a river of sewage blended with lovely toilet cleaner and air freshener all in one. It's more cleaner innit?

GENGIS: Indubitably. I'm pleased to see you are still taking care of the environment. (*He inhales deeply. Chatting idly as they proceed to his quarters.*) That's great. I swear by it. The great thing about a good air freshener is that in real emergencies you can stick it right up your arse.

AUNTY: Now, this is your boudoir.

GENGIS: How dare you! This is nothing but a smear of filth on the ground. And there are tens of other girls.

AUNTY: I'm afraid that's how Philippinos live.

GENGIS: It's disgusting.

AUNTY: Now, I have to inspect your knickers regularly to check you have your period and to detect any signs of sexual arousal, which is not allowed.

GENGIS: What a shame. Why not?

AUNTY: We can't employ pregnant women, they take up too much room, fart too often and then they want time off to give birth.

GENGIS: I promise that if I do give birth I'll put it straight down the lavatory.

AUNTY: Oh alright then.

GENGIS: Now, how about my wages?

AUNTY: Only after you've worked. And after I've made the deductions which I want in advance. You owe me three dollars.

GENGIS: Deductions? For what?

AUNTY: Accommodation, toilet cleaner expenses, company disco – workers not invited – golf course, country club, swimming pool, jaccuzi, net surfer lounge, aerobics club, Christmas box.

GENGIS: Hm. I can't wait.

AUNTY: Not for you Dummy, for us. You'd better get in to work or you'll be late and we'll sack you and you'll have to walk back home to where your village used to be – it's fifty miles without a packed lunch.

GENGIS walks on.

GENGIS: Uncle! Is that you?

UNCLE: I cannot tell a lie.

GENGIS: Well, I'm sure surprised to see you here. Are you working for the Americans too?

UNCLE: Only in a postmodern ironic sort of way.

GENGIS: I came here to oppose America.

UNCLE: America isn't a place, it's a state of mind.

GENGIS: Gee Unk, it's kinda confusing. You're exploiting slave labour, having an easy ride on the backs of the helpless, you're a coward and a collaborator…and yet you wear really cool designer clothes, and you look so cool.

UNCLE: Even we top executives have to look cool these days.

GENGIS: Everyone these days, all your favourite stars and all your favourite heroes and all your favourite friends; they're all in on it. I shall have to fight on alone.

UNCLE: I think you'll find you've got rather a lot of overtime to do this week. You may be too busy.

GENGIS: Hang on, overtime? Overtime? I already work fourteen hours a day!

UNCLE: We've got a big order for anti-slavery T-shirts.

XIX

GENGIS: My fingers are worn to the bone, look!

UNCLE: Very nasty. Now, may I check your knickers?

GENGIS: Again?

UNCLE: We must be vigilant against abuses. Let me help you there…

GENGIS: Thank you squire, most kind… You don't feel that's an infringement of my, you know, private parts?

UNCLE: Oh no, no. It's all global now. You have no private parts; what's yours is mine.

GENGIS: Global? In what way??

UNCLE: Well, em… We're all One.

GENGIS: Aha. Does that mean we take care not just of our own corner where we live, and our own people, but of the whole planet and all the people in it lovingly, as if we're all the same?

UNCLE: Em…no it means we use the whole planet as a toilet and *all* the people in it as toilet attendants, giving *everyone* the opportunity to spray some air freshener, or even, hey, who knows, to manufacture it in their own back yards. And then, after they have saved up, they can *buy* a tin of air freshener and stick it up their arseholes and spray, thus creating a fresh and homely environment for when we next want to sodomise them.

GENGIS: Opportunity knocks.

UNCLE: Opportunity enters without knocking.

XX

GENGIS: Uncle, I'm shocked, you'll never guess what I've just seen piled up out the back of this factory?

UNCLE: What is it my little flower of the Orient?

GENGIS: Hundreds of my Nooses, in a great mountain.

UNCLE: Well, that's wonderful Gengis.

GENGIS: But don't you understand? What I want to know is – what are they doing here?

UNCLE: This is where we make them.

GENGIS: Is it? I thought it was home produce, I thought it was jobs for the boys, I thought it was employment UK.

UNCLE: Not exactly Gengis…no.

GENGIS: You'll never guess what else I've seen.

UNCLE: What is it, O inscrutable lotus blossom.

GENGIS: The workers are starting to wear these nooses for their own pleasure and delectation.

UNCLE: No!

GENGIS: Yes.

UNCLE: Can they afford them?

GENGIS: You know how they love to make little sacrifices to be able to look great. Anyway, scores of them are hanging from nooses along the electric perimeter fencing. You'll have no nimble-fingered labour left at this rate.

UNCLE: Hmm… I'll see to it. Meanwhile, show us your knickers.

XXI

UNCLE: How's work?

GENGIS: I'm excited to be part of growth and progress in the Philippines.

UNCLE: Aren't we all? (*Emits an insane laugh of hysterical greed, which he discretely suppresses.*) Yes, yes, injections of cash into the economy, brings wealth and health.

GENGIS: Yes, where there is poverty we shall bring prosperity, where there is ignorance we shall bring craftiness, where there is hopelessness we shall bring ambition, where there are farms we shall bring golf courses.

UNCLE: Fancy joining me and the other subcontractors for a round? You can be my caddy.

GENGIS: With pleasure, I like to supplement my wages whenever possible.

UNCLE: I'll pay you fifteen cents.

GENGIS: That's more than my hourly rate!

UNCLE: Think nothing of it. What's that in your pocket?

GENGIS: It's my new girlfriend and fellow worker.

UNCLE: What's her name?

GENGIS: Thumbelina McMarcos.

UNCLE: She's very small.

GENGIS: That's right, but she works very hard.

There is a squeak from GENGIS's breast pocket. It is THUMBELINA talking.

THUMBELINA: Squeak, squeak!

GENGIS: (*To THUMBELINA.*) What's that you say?

THUMBELINA: Squeak, squeak!

GENGIS: Oh, you say you used to work on the farm that used to be where the Resource Centre and helicopter pad lounge now is?

THUMBELINA: Squeak, squeak!

GENGIS: And although they pay you less and treat you like dogs and work you like slaves until you drop dead, or wear out, or reach the age of twenty-four, you've got no choice?

THUMBELINA: Squeak, squeak!

GENGIS: That's just about the size of it, she says.

UNCLE: She's very articulate isn't she?

GENGIS: I don't just love her for her tight little fanny, you know.

UNCLE: You might be putting words into her mouth.

GENGIS: You're joking, I can't get anything into her mouth, I've tried.

UNCLE: She looks like a trouble-maker to me.

GENGIS: Hm, you reckon? But less trouble I bet than her father, who expects a living wage.

UNCLE: Well alright, but I'm warning you, if she gets pregnant she'll be dismissed immediately.

THUMBELINA: Squeak, squeak!

GENGIS: She says one day she'll start a union, then you'll be sorry!

UNCLE: On that day the factory will move to Kakastan, never to return.

THUMBELINA: Squeak.

GENGIS: Good riddance.

UNCLE: Well, there's gratitude for you. What did I tell you?

THUMBELINA: Squeak!

GENGIS: She says that she knows that when the Lord of Heaven, Mickey McMouse®, the Great American God and his Princess Barbie® hear of this, all wrong-doers will be punished. We the girls of the happy tax holiday centre in the Philippines and the world over live in hope of that happy moment for we know the Lord Mickey® loves everybody everywhere!

THUMBELINA: Squeak!

GENGIS: She says Coca Cola® is the real thing and she has read that she is well worth it and it's her life and that all she has to do is think different...ly and it will be a way of life and a solution for the whole planet...

THUMBELINA: Squeak!

GENGIS: Beware you wicked old style employer, for
Nike® and Adidas® will come in the sky to save us, and
IBM® will put to death all dogs such as you. Sherlock
Holmes® too will come to reclaim his hats and shoes.
You will be detected and we will fly to America® land of
the free and equal, far from the cruelties of this sad little
land of ours. Justice® and freedom® and free burgers
for all babies in the womb®. Salvation®, from the
brands you can trust®.

UNCLE: She's got the right idea, this chick. She has a
simple trusting nature. Is she wearing one of my T-shirts,
by any chance?

GENGIS: Sure is! Three weeks wages worth of pure
identity! I can hardly see her under it – its really rather
alluring.

XXII

*GENGIS comes whistling to work and discovers everything is gone.
Where the factory was is now a black hole.*

GENGIS: I don't understand; where the factory once was is
now just a black hole. Thumbelina, where are you??

He calls to her in the emptiness. It echoes as in a forest clearing.

Have they gone over-night, leaving nothing but a
training shoe, a bottle of air freshener, and a Sherlock
Holmes hat?

He has discovered these items and he fondles them.

THUMBELINA: (*Who has been squashed into the mud.*)
Squeak, squeak!

GENGIS: Thumbelina! What has happened to you? What?? You've been squashed into the mud by the removal lorries? You tried to block their path?

THUMBELINA: Squeak, squeak!

GENGIS: 'Come back and exploit us some more,' you said, 'build more bigger better factories, we won't disappoint you, we'll work even harder to please your every whim, and help you live your pointless empty greedy stupid lives, we'll help you flush away what's left of the planet, and we'll live those stupid lives with you, and we'll flush away anything you like, but please don't go, please don't go, we didn't mean to be difficult!'? Is that what you said?

THUMBELINA: Squeak.

GENGIS: But my poor darling Thumbelina, that's like a girl calling to her rapist 'Come back and marry me'!

THUMBELINA: Squeak.

GENGIS: That's about the size of it? Hmm. But now look at you? What happened?

THUMBELINA: Squeak, squeak.

GENGIS: They drove the truck over you?

THUMBELINA: (*Feebly.*) Squeak.

GENGIS: Oh, my poor little Thumbelina! Forgive me!

Enter UNCLE carrying a set of golf clubs and a small suitcase.

UNCLE: Still loitering about the place eh Gengis? Mind the security guards don't feed you to their dogs.

GENGIS: Where is everything?

UNCLE: We're moving to China. Spiralling labour costs have left us no choice. In China we don't pay them anything at all, and when they get old or worn out the workers are simply liquidated and replaced with new ones.

GENGIS: That's horrible.

UNCLE: Yes, but it keeps the cost of a pair of trainers down to around a hundred and twenty pounds.

GENGIS: You ought to be ashamed.

UNCLE: I quite agree, which is why I'm so pleased we have managed to rid our country of these terrible Dickensian-style practises, and moved Britain into the next millennium as a modern efficient and streamline economy that can sustain the lifestyle of today's kinda people. By the way can I check your knickers?

GENGIS: Leave my bloody knickers alone! You've squashed Thumbelina!

UNCLE: I never touched you.

GENGIS: And now she's dying, in the mud. Look at her. Do you think its right that a young Philippino girl should die to support Auntie's terrible taste in lifestyle choices?

UNCLE: I'm looking, and what I'm seeing says to me – yesterday. Just that. Yesterday. I'm only interested in tomorrow. New horizons for a new world.

XXIII

Back in Britain.

GENGIS: Gee its great to be back in London, England. Meet my Dad, Soul Prestige, and my Mum, Vicky Slimming.

UNCLE: Howdedoody.

GENGIS: We grew up in a culturally deprived area. We had more money than sense. We weren't poor but we were working class...

UNCLE: Oh dear how sad; it's the children I feel sorry for.

VICKY: Yeah well, it's each to his own, innit? Weren't poor? We was rich!

PRESTIGE: Shut it Vicky love.

VICKY: Suit yourself. I've got to go and get some work done on my bum-cheeks, they're just enormous today.

PRESTIGE: Shelf it Vicky love.

VICKY: Suit yourself. It's like I say, each to his own.

PRESTIGE: Shut it Vicky love. Let me talk to this geezer then we'll blow, okay?

VICKY: Suit yourself, its like I say –

PRESTIGE: Vicky! Stow it! – (*Friendly.*) Now what's your problem mate?

UNCLE: Nothing. I'm very pleased to meet you. I hear em... I hear you're Gengis's parents.

PRESTIGE: Yeah, that's right. So what's all this then?

UNCLE: This? Oh it's a theatre play.

PRESTIGE: Oh yeah? My brother-in-law was in a theatre play. Musical. Yeah he was the lead role actually, in the West End, bought hisself a house in Enfield. I didn't see it myself. Now, he said they was a load of pooftahs, every one of them.

UNCLE: Yes, that's right.

PRESTIGE: Well it's like I say, each to his own innit?

VICKY: There's nothing wrong with pooftahs, Clive.

PRESTIGE: Didn't say there was did I? (*To UNCLE.*) No, he said they was all at it. But like I say, it's each to his own innit?

UNCLE: …I just wanted to ask about Gengis's childhood.

PRESTIGE: Yeah well. I'll tell you what. You arst your questions and I'll drive Vicky to the gym, and if you've got any more problems just come to me and I'll sort it out. You've got my mobile?

UNCLE: 07777197483493293293939939349309840874848?

PRESTIGE: That's it. I'll be up Hoddeston, but I'll drive down, …now, Traffic, centre of London…em well, it'll take about ten minutes.

VICKY: (*Mock reproachful but thrilled in her knickers.*) The way you drive yeah.

PRESTIGE: Stow it Vicky. So that's alright then?

UNCLE: That's fine.

PRESTIGE: No, its like I say. They were alright, like; but they was all queer. And the audience. But they are, you know. Dressing up like girls and that. No I've got nothing against them. My mum was queer. And my brother in law, Sequin, he was bent as a 'air pin actually, that's why he was in it… And er, well my sister, she's got to be, ain't she Vicky?

VICKY: Oh yeah!

PRESTIGE: (*To UNCLE.*) Yeah. She eats them er…little ham sandwiches, d'you know what I mean? (*Laughs.*)

VICKY laughs.

They both laugh till they nearly wet theirselves.

VICKY: No, he loves her really don't you Prestige?

PRESTIGE: Yeah, I love her really. If anyone so much as lay a finger on her, I tell ya, two minutes, me and me mates, baseball bats; there'd be nothing left. Just takes one phone call.

VICKY: Yeah, he loves her really. He's just an old softie aren't ya, Prestige?

PRESTIGE: Yeah, I am really. I've always been like it. Just an old softie. Vicky always says that about me, don't ya Vicky?

VICKY: Yeah.

PRESTIGE: No, in fact that's what they say about me, isn't it?

VICKY: What?

PRESTIGE: They say actually that if I wasn't such a hard nut you'd think I was a pooftah.

VICKY: (*To UNCLE, eager to convince.*) Yeah they do actually.

PRESTIGE: 'Cause I'm so gentle.

VICKY: Yeah, he's really gentle. Where do they say that then?

PRESTIGE: Down the pub they say it.

VICKY: Yeah well, it's like I say, each to his own.

PRESTIGE: Don't start, Vicky.

VICKY: What?

PRESTIGE: Have you got your tights on, cause we're gonna be late.

VICKY: Of course I have got my tights on. Cheeky!

PRESTIGE: You never know. Come on you slag.

VICKY: Speak for yourself.

75

UNCLE: (*Aside to GENGIS.*) So Gengis, this is your Mum and Dad eh?

GENGIS: Yes, well sort of.

UNCLE: What do you mean sort of?

GENGIS: They're younger than me, Uncle. Couldn't you see?

UNCLE: It's so hard to tell these days. They seemed so mature.

GENGIS: Yeah well Vicky Slimming is in her twenties, and Soul Prestige did the discos in Hoxton ten years ago. He made a fortune.

UNCLE: Hm I see. So why did you introduce them as your parents?

GENGIS: God, Uncle! It's a spiritual search.

UNCLE: Cobblers.

GENGIS: I wish I came from good honest stock like that.

UNCLE: Don't we all.

GENGIS: (*To VICKY SLIMMING and SOUL PRESTIGE.*) Actually, Mum, Dad, I've brought my new fiancee to meet you. Her name is Thumbelina.

THUMBELINA: Squeak, squeak.

GENGIS: She says she's deeply honoured and has been waiting for this moment, it is the culmination of her life so far.

PRESTIGE: Yeah, sweet.

VICKY: Gengis, a word?

GENGIS: Yes?

VICKY: I'm not being funny or nothing, but I think she's too fucking small, alright? Don't get me wrong, yeah?

GENGIS: In what way is she too small?

VICKY: I'm not being funny or nothin', yeah? but these days, if you're not the normal size you ain't really fitting in.

GENGIS: Admittedly I found her squashed in the mud, but now she is recovered. She's been preparing herself to meet you.

VICKY: Yeah, fine, I'm not knockin' that, yeah? but if she wants to get along with people, she's gonna 'ave to be more larger, do y'get me?

GENGIS: She's worked all her short life and she's undernourished and shy.

VICKY: Yeah. No, look, I'm not knockin that, yeah? don't get me wrong or nothin' but as you know, I've been around the world twice, so there's no pulling the wool over my eyes with all this, 'O I'm foreign, make excuses for me,' lark, because I've seen it all before.

GENGIS: You've been to Toremelinos.

VICKY: I worked for a travel agent's yeah, don't forget that.

GENGIS: Excuse me, Thumbelina is speaking.

THUMBELINA: Squeak, squeak.

GENGIS: She says she can see from the size of your arse that you must be a very important person. In her village only the elders were allowed to have arses that big. She says you are a goddess and she's proud to have given the best years of her life to stitch the seams of those clothes you're wearing – for indeed she recognises them, they were put together in her factory. She is happy to die in that knowledge.

VICKY: Tell her that's very nice but I got these in Wood Green Shopping City actually, and they're real, not cheap imitations, thank you very much. Now if she doesn't mind some of us have got work to do, yeah?

THUMBELINA: Squeak.

GENGIS: She says, may she respectfully observe that the real ones, as you call them, are also cheap imitations so to speak, you don't make nothing here no more, your clothes have the blood and sweat of her cousins all over them so don't pretend to yourself.

VICKY: Whatever, yeah? Clive, tell 'em will ya?

PRESTIGE: What is it, babes?

VICKY: She's buggin' me about my leggings but I got them in Wood Green.

PRESTIGE: (*To THUMBELINA.*) Listen love, we're not political, okay? There y'are, sorted.

VICKY: I'm not being funny or nothing, but tell your little friend – we don't like trouble, yeah?

PRESTIGE: Leave it Vicky.

UNCLE: Can Aunty have a lift in your giant Range Roover?

PRESTIGE: No room mate, we've got to pick up our kid from nursery, and take him to gymnastics. Then he's got football, then French, then Nuclear physics, then Judo, then he's got glass blowing, and personal relationships, then sailing, then parking, shopping, and feeding the monkeys, ballroom dancing, then jive-talking, and police baiting, and job application skills, innit. No room mate.

UNCLE: Can she run behind?

PRESTIGE: It's a free country.

VICKY SLIMMING and SOUL PRESTIGE go off with their car keys a-jangle.

THUMBELINA: Squeak.

GENGIS: 'Can we go to America now?' Whatever for?

THUMBELINA: Squeak, squeak.

GENGIS: If I don't take you to America, the land of Justice, you won't believe that I love you? But Thumbelina, you've got it all wrong. And besides, according to Uncle, America isn't a place it's state of mind.

THUMBELINA: Squeak.

GENGIS: He's a liar? But I couldn't possibly go to America; their TV is atrocious and the car parks are so big you end up walking miles just to buy a pint of milk. Can't we stay here?

THUMBELINA: Squeak.

GENGIS: Love is nice but America is better??

THUMBELINA: Squeak.

GENGIS: It's the holy people, and you also want to be free from exploitation at last. Don't I believe in the future? Come on baby let's rock and roll?

THUMBELINA: Squeak, squeak.

GENGIS: You can't live without hope? the world needs hope?

THUMBELINA: Squeak.

GENGIS: What's that?, a rainbow in the sky? Oh, yes, I can see...something...

THUMBELINA: Squeak.

GENGIS: The rainbow is where America is? No I don't want to face life without hope. No I wouldn't rob you of that.

THUMBELINA: Squeak

GENGIS: Yes, it is a lovely rainbow.

Enter UNCLE, in a kind 'service at table' uniform.

UNCLE: Hi guys. Coffee anyone?

THUMBELINA: Squeak, squeak.

GENGIS: Yes, Uncle, thanks. Thumbelina is dying for a cup.

UNCLE: Great rainbow® huh?

GENGIS: Yes, it's neat.

THUMBELINA: Squeak.

GENGIS: Yes, she says it's neat too.

UNCLE: It's part of what we call the hope experience; we find most of our customers don't just like it, they are beginning to find that it helps them face the disappointment of life itself, and hey, who knows, maybe to dream, to hope, to plan, something better.

GENGIS: That's swell.

UNCLE: Is it art? Is it philosophy, or is it just something spiritual. Who knows? We just call it coffee – a cup of Rainbow® coffee – Enjoy.

The End.